The Fragrance of Dust

Haiku Stories Poems

James Norton

Alba Publishing

Published by Alba Publishing
P O Box 266, Uxbridge
UB9 5NX, United Kingdom
www.albapublishing.com

A catalogue record for this book is available from the British Library

ISBN: 978-0-9551254-8-5

Edited, designed and typeset by Kim Richardson
Cover image: James Norton
Printed by Clondalkin Group, Glasnevin, Ireland

10 9 8 7 6 5 4 3 2 1

Contents

Introduction

This collection gathers together haiku, haibun and poems written over a twenty year span.

In 1991 I began writing again after a fallow period of similar duration. It was the discovery of haiku which prompted me to begin anew. Or rather the rediscovery, because sometime in the late 60's I had come across the following lines and been very struck by them, without knowing quite why: sitting quietly/doing nothing/Spring comes/the grass grows by itself.

Haiku is now a very well known form, written in many languages world-wide. Many are attracted to it as a literary exercise, a challenge in conciseness. Others sense that there may be more to its 'lessness' than that. A few may choose to follow *haiku no michi*, a means of liberation in itself, albeit modest and momentary. At its most effective, haiku is "a tiny coiled spring that can release fleeting but subtle insights into how life is". Yet this will only be so, it seems to me, if one eschews conformity to notions of a rigid 5-7-5 syllable 3-line formula confined to 'objective sketching' in the manner of a photographic image or mere nature-note. Even a slight knowledge of the tradition shows that the Japaneses masters didn't limit themselves so.

Haibun are more talkative members of the haiku family, and is a new genre now establishing itself in the West under many guises. The great classic is Matsuo Basho's *The Narrow Road to the Deep North*. Included here are examples of my use of it in that form, a sub-species of travel writing, perhaps. I have felt free to experiment with it in other ways, too. Likewise the sequencing of haiku as I have done here draws on a tradition pre-dating 'stand-alone' haiku. A native inspiration here has been translations of early Irish nature lyrics, often the marginalia of monks, resonating deeply across time and space with the Eastern contemplative spirit.

But why confine oneself to poetic forms originating in the East? Occasion and theme impel their own shaping, and suitable responses need be found, from whatever source: hence the poems.

As to how to order such diverse material, I've opted for a loose chronology roughly corresponding to my wanderings during this period (1991-2011), outer and inner journey echoing each other. An exception to this time-line is the Three Abandonments section, which points back to a much earlier period which seemed important to include as an acknowledgement of where I was coming from.

Most of it is previously unpublished except in 'fugitive' forms—the occasional pamphlet, exchanges with fellow travellers and the like. A little has been, so from my *Words on the Wind* (Waning Moon Press 1997) the Owl House Days section touches on that. Some too from *Pilgrim Foxes*, co-authored with Ken Jones and Sean O'Connor (Pilgrim Press 2001), various haibun and haiku seemed worth re-printing. Thanks to the editors of *Blithe Spirit, Haiku Presence, Shamrock, Snapshot Press, Contemporary Haibun Online* and various international anthologies for haiku published; also BBC Wildlife Poetry Award 1992 (for 'rook rensaku') and Genjuan Haibun Competition 2012 (for 'Yeh Go I').

I am indebted to Ken Jones for, among many kindnesses, his generous foreword to this collection; to George Marsh for invaluable support and constructive criticism over many years, especially with the poems; to Kim Richardson of Alba Publishing for making this collection possible; to ever-supportive friends Tom Matthews, Sean O'Connor of *Haiku Spirit*, Maeve O'Sullivan and Gilles Fabre of Haiku Ireland, and fellow members of the Redthread group; most especially to my dharma teachers Venerable Chögyam Trungpa Rinpoche and Sakyong Mipham, themselves great poets, and much more: to all, a deep bow. May basic goodness dawn!

James Norton
Dublin
May 2012

Foreword by Ken Jones

For many years I have appreciated Jim Norton's haiku, poems and haibun. As I learned how sustaining they could be in difficult times, I have been careful to keep them close at hand. I turn to them in moments of quiet reflection, and so often life feels that little bit easier.

> Quiet now
>   the street of angry voices
>   where we dream

Now all are gathered together here for others to share—browsing, exploring, enjoying, and, yes, finding inspiration. They do their work subtly and lightly, and typically with a certain lean austerity. But about most of them there is a delicate, understated tenderness. I am reminded of what Goethe said about the gift that such poets have to offer to us: "When man in his agony is dumb, we have God's gift to utter what we suffer". Sometimes this compassion is explicit: here the poet finds himself in yet another cramped room in some lodging house near the Guinness brewery in Dublin:

> coughing
>   and the stranger upstairs
>   coughs too

At other times it is just the expression of our common humanity that says enough—a poignancy deeply felt when our minds are still:

> between tenements
>   red ball of sun:
>   she hobbles on home

It is said that some live to write poetry, whilst others write poetry to live. Jim Norton undoubtedly is one of the latter. As a distinctively haiku poet he always leaves enough space for our own imagination, as readers, to flower and to move us.

Notice to quit:
the musician's violin
snug in its case

There, too, are the moments of breathtaking beauty—

In the cries of swans
the winter lake finds voice
reeds white-feathered

And then we may turn the page to be pulled up short by some sudden moment of ecstasy, even in the humble kitchen garden:-

Oh quick, the sun
the fiery sun
sets beneath the bean-rows

This collection is exceptional in offering, as well as haiku, such a rich variety of other writing: linked sequences of haiku, poems in western forms, and a fascinating new genre called haibun—a blend of haiku and story at which Norton excels. Here we find outer and inner journeying mirroring each other across a wide canvas, from his native Ireland to Wales, Spain, Poland.

A seasoned Buddhist practitioner, he finds inspiration by travelling the way, and equally in Christian and secular settings. His is a spirituality never explicitly stated yet always subtly informing the work, springing up where least expected—

Sound of a spoon
striking an empty bowl:
that's it!

Ken Jones, Cwm Rheidol, December 2011

[Ken Jones is a senior teacher with the Western Chan Fellowship, has published several volumes of haiku and haibun, and is co-editor of Contemporary Haibun OnLine]

OWL HOUSE DAYS

She walks her horses
  up the long hill, three heads
    bowed to the rain

                    Through the long night
                    they have leaned on each other
                    the fork and the spade

August heat—
faint click of pine cones
opening as we part

                    The news —
                      across rippling wheat
                        shadows scythe

Leaving the Owl House
(for JT)

My love & I
  in a stripped house:

Forgotten anything?
  Tulip petals on a bare shelf.

Fledgling cries.
  Bending low
    the burden of blossom.

Never did fix that gate.
    Let honeysuckle bind it.

Rook rensaku
(for TL)

Roar of the beaters from the wood
   in the garden leaves fly
   from our rakes

in the mud of hunters' tracks
   wildly in all directions
   pheasant clawprints

after the shoot
   the winter field
   silent and empty

   a wounded rook
      in withered cornstalks
      hunched and impassive

         tending the bird
      transforms you into a boy
         fatherly sounds of comfort

         indifferent to food
   claws gripping a finger
      he submits to stroking

my gaze is drawn
into the pool of his clear eye
shock of my tiny reflection

left to himself
in his own time he flies
beyond motion and hurt

bury me in the sky
tucked in the fork of a high tree
beak to the black north

winter light
burning me into the blue

The work done
    and well done, too,
now put it to the candle.
Let no-one know what passed between
the moon, the moth, the pencil.

        While sane folk snore
           restless legs must roam
    and in the silence of the hammer-ponds
    unearth the ore
                assay the clinker.

THREE ABANDONMENTS

Portrait of an Ox and Unicorn
(for B)

Half a life ago
When youth burned blue as a cutter's tool,
Two inseparable companions
Rattled the cage of every rule,
Trod the edge to vertigo.

We woke to strangeness, out of season,
Knew no antecedents.
Oddity our grudging alias,
indifference our shaky alibi.
Gallery visits, smuggled books sustained us.
And the night-time tracery of vision.

Luminous wakings flashed;
Ideas sudden as rockets, images
Fragmentary and precious,
Intoxicant, dangerous.
Hubris mounted on the red rush.

We stole no sacred fires.
All or nothing became nothing.
On crept the slow chill of years.
Now strike a light, and see them drawn
In a painted cave your ox, my unicorn.

Crazy Diamond
(a myth of my self)

Swaddled in my country bed
comes to me suddenly—

there was blood in the air
those days when he walked the Liberties
from end to end, senses blazing.

He had slain a god
and a red sun roared down Pig Street.
Each cobbled yard, decrepit street

flung open the mystery,
made all things possible.
All lay bare beneath his blade.

He laughed, and darted dagger-bright
into the interstices, hair streaming.
And each crystal node disclosed

mere permutations of an empty play,
centreless and without fringe.
The ground gave way beneath his feet.

Then he knew terror.
Undoing all undid himself.
He could not lick that honeyed blade.

Wandered, and his claws grew.
Came on a cave, lived out of sight.
And as the roaring died away

a small voice sounded:
    seek now
                the uncreate.

Blinking, he ventured outside,
and came upon blue iris
rooted in mud.

Mute Celestial

Into black the amber pours
The ripeness of an afternoon.
A bald head gleams, an upraised glass
Sparkles into emptiness. Take out the pen.

Its shadow creeps across the page
Like a gnomon fingering a dial.
Wait for it—perhaps this time
Voice the mute celestial.

Fold the paper, put the pen away,
Hapless un-annunciate.
The little thing too huge to say;
Mumble thanks and slink outside.

On the corner, in the rain
The promise offers yet again.
Smells of fruit and flowers float
Above the hawker's gutteral shout.

Buy a loaf and eat it on the way.

DOUBLIN' BACK

Icy new year
at the tip of bull island
crescent moon

Salt whitened
remains of a sand-hare
spirited away

The cliff path—
seeing how it disappears
I love it more

Sea light
outracing the wind
a raptor

Brú

Such a sky—
the ache of loss is answered
and returned entire

It was soon after I returned, and savouring the pleasures of rediscovering the old amongst the strangely new, my wanderings led me back here, to the old Fever Hospital. I looked with great curiosity through the railings, remembering my grandmother's stories of the months I spent here, an infant confined in isolation, numbered like the others so that parents, prohibited from visiting, might learn of our condition by looking in the weekly newspaper notice, the heading of the column in which each number was placed indicating the prognosis. Now it serves to see us out.

A handbell is ringing:
beneath boughs heavy with blossom
old men linger.

The sound breaks
across the hostel grounds
petals scatter.

The neighbour
gathers up her child, hurrying,
slams the red door.

Brú: The dictionary gives two meanings for this Gaelic word (1) hostel (2) press, shove, crush; pressure as in blood; bruise.

Wings

Near Basin Lane a tethered pony noses a circle of bare earth. Crystals from a shattered windscreen sparkle in the gutter. On the pavement a huddle of boys, one in the middle, hands cupped. They crowd in to look, voices hushed, tone awed. What has he found? What has made them leave off tormenting cats, setting fire to skips, throwing stones at the mad woman's door?

Fluttering by
something never seen before
is caught and held

Poppies

Now thousands of houses have sprung from the fields and on this rawest edge of the city, a group of recovering addicts have come along to try their hand at haiku. We go outside to walk and maybe find some.

At the cross-roads a decrepit caravan is parked on the verge. A man stands in the doorway, watching. Big man. He's mental, say the others, even his own won't have him. They move on. His dogs rush toward me. Strangely, I'm unafraid. He watches as I fondle them, approaches unsteadily, extends a huge hand, mumbles thanks for... bein' kind to the dogs. We exchange place-names. Both of us are from somewhere.

I rejoin the group. We walk beyond the burnt-out cars, discover a stream brimming with water-cress, listen to a blackbird. The sunset's magnificence is heart-breaking.

> By Lady's Well
> crowned with poppies
> a heap of junk

Sparks from a charnel-ground

They sing at night
   the blackbirds of Rialto
      never to be seen

                        my window open
                           all the sounds of the night
                           all that is left unsaid

she is hammering
and calling *Joe...Joe...*
but Joe is gone

single now
I throw away
the avocado stones

checking my face
where the mirror isn't
a stranger grins back

dawn raid—
  naked in the doorway
    nothing to say

locked myself out:
  my troublesome neighbour
    knows just the right kick

coughing
  and the stranger upstairs
    coughs too

look at it—
    battered old heater:
        here, let me warm you!

between tenements
  red ball of sun:
    she hobbles on home

quiet now
  the street of angry voices
    where we dream

hours before dawn
in the hospital grounds
to whom does the blackbird
call so sweetly?

snow is falling on the bell that never rings

The Magdalens' Bench

The inscription reads:

> *Sit:*
> *reflect here upon their lives.*

May heaven strike me if I weep, hell
If I do not.

> A wren is hurrying
> between the blossom and the thorn.

*[Magdalens: Unmarried mothers incarcerated and made to labour in
laundries owned and run by religious orders.]*

On the Circular Road

He left me alone to make up my mind. One felt the weight of all three storeys bearing down upon it, a basement flatlet offering little light, one barred window, weedy yard out back. Still, there was a rightness to the layout, tiny yet complete, gloomy but clean. Airless though. Buried alive. What age of a man are you, he'd asked in that blunt country way. Afraid I might die on him, stink up the place. Above, someone pulls the plug, or flushes a loo. Down it cascades, rattling the pipework.

Just this—
entering the sound:
home

Sandscript

> Lost to sight
> a seabird's piping
> pierces home

Nasturtiums crowd the porch, spilling orange light through the open door. The grass is seldom cut and snails abound. I enjoy a spacious upper room with two tall windows and a creaking floor. To walk across it is a conversation, the better part of which is listening, as brick and lath and joist settle with little groans and sighs into what they are.

> A garlic clove:
> into the dark

Baby William Butler Yeats was wheeled in a carriage through these streets. Young Stephen Dedalus strode into eternity along this strand. There Bloom ever wanders, ogles Gertie while his Molly plays. Which is real, who imagines?

> Herons
> mirrored in sky-pools
> ruffled, rippled

> Hand in hand
> two tiny figures
> cross immensity

The sea disappears eastward each day and comes back speaking in tongues, cries of seabirds voice unsayables, the waters riddle answers in sandscript and each night erase.

> Notice to quit:
> the musician's violin
> snug in its case

33

Out of the Blue

The evening is warm and clear, but something else is happening: sensing a change in the air I hurry through the streets to the shoreline. Out of the blue

> Sea mist—
> gathered up in it
> the floating world

Between the wasteland and the strand, drifting in a state dream-like but with senses heightened, feeling each droplet, turning about in wonder, out of insubstantiality forms manifest. Slabs of concrete bristling with rusty iron float into view, dissolve. Dripping silver, a toothy stand of teasels cards the fleecy wraiths.

> On the shoreline
> man and heron
> swallowed whole

From the mouth of the bay beyond, voicing inexpressible longing

> Cloud-wrapped
> in utter stillness
> the foghorn lows

In response the thought arises: I need go no further, say no more. Here is condensed all I have searched for, ever-receeding yet everywhere at once, ungraspable yet soaking me through and through. Again the South Bull sounds, and out of the depths a sea-calf answers.

Turning for home along the track, so deliciously contrary the crunching sound I look down in delight.

> In its own time
> a snail with horns erect
> floats over the cinders

Sea-rusted
      its job now
            is to be
rich & strange
         and useless

Dark water
blown by the wind
lit gulls

               Plovers on salt grass
               which way are you headed
               in the early dark?

Between Bridges

A Sunday morning in early July after a night of warm rain, clouds promising more, the air tumescent with scents. At Lansdowne Bridge on impulse cycle upstream along the Dodder—*An Dothra,* the Flood—towards Ball's Bridge.

Brown waters in a green tunnel, here smooth, there breaking, melodious chatter of salt meeting sweet, low tide exposing bladder-wrack where ducks doze and feed.

At this hour, few up and about, local sabbath-keepers, and some minders of the moment—

> Voices low
> three excited japanese
> peer into the shallows

Under the railway arch, another world. Fouled newpapers, odours of stale piss. Transport of smells.

Short pants, school toilets, fear and faecination. Bloom at stool above the rising. Buddleia, valerian, extravagances pink and purple rooted in the stones. Dusty fragrances.

Waited for her here an age ago.

The Sweep. I'll stake my all on it. Bated breath. A nurse stands starch-stiff, holds aloft the winning ticket. Son behold thy mother and her best friend May, leaning on the river wall, smoking Sweet Afton, day's work done.

In mid-river, so close I stare into its unblinking eye, a heron stands, scratching its gullet with the long claw, black crest feathers erected in a fan, exercising its oesophagus in long fish-swallowing gulps. Bends its neck and hunches, watching the flow.

A Sunday painter stands by his easel, brush poised. Water colours.

Exchange nods. Bids me good morning. Ulster accent. Down for a bit of peace and quiet, month that's in it—Glorious Twelfth. Risking trespass I remark: that's a sight worth seeing, and gesture to the heron. Looks better this way I think...composition. Gestures a diagonal to the poplars beyond. The bird is relegated to the lower corner. Select your realisms.

A man leans on the parapet of Ball's Bridge, watching both of us, or so it seems. Drawing closer I see that he is roughly dressed, nut-brown with a leathery face made darker by the shadow of his cap. Foreign looking, seaman-like. Loquacious now, I venture: Worth watching, eh? He stares back at me, inscrutable. I wonder has he English. Somewhere beyond words, he turns and resumes his watch.

> Absorbed
> he is with the heron
> on the turning tide

[The Sweep: Irish Hospital Sweepstakes]

Knockree

Switch off. Sit motionless a while. Drifts of mist settle on the windscreen, gather into beads, pool their weights, slide down in crooked courses, stop, start again.

Others here before me, a dozen cars emptied into mountain quiet, a presence absorbing all, an absence palpable, sways and whispers.

Now as then, waft and tang, moist air releasing after heat, spicy sweetness of gorse, aromatics of crushed bracken, pine-ooze, oily reek of sheep.

Find the gap, the meadow sloping up, fine grasses yellowed early, feathery seed-heads, uncut thistles elbow high, purpling.

Summer evenings here the rug is spread, we gather round a windup gramophone, cavort, sing along: *He walks the bloody tower/with his head/ tucked/underneath his arm/at the midnight hour....*

City children holidaying. There I am in sepia, seated on a donkey, its ears back, not pleased. No more I am myself, braving it, but her arm around me and she smiling. Happy then.

A two-roomed cottage, loaned to us by one-eyed Uncle Jack. Turning the pages of damp picture-books while rain hammered on the tin roof. Emerging into sunlit vibrant silence. In the clang of a bucket the mountain rings out.

From across the valley a soft roar, cascading between Ton Duff and Maulin. Wonder, on being told its name: O'Toole's Buttermilk.

In the hearth a nail, long, square-shouldered, hand-forged. That'll do.

>   roofless
>   all that was in it
>   flown

WESTERLIES

Ox Mountain Trail

In the summer of 1998 and again the following Easter, I travelled west to the Carmelite hermitage of Holy Hill in Co. Sligo, seeking common ground between the lotus and the cross.

Across the interior
cows knee-deep in buttercups
quiet old fears

fleetingly, a hare:
first smile of the day

dark hills
and on them darker patches.
I have gone too far

under Ox Mountain
cliffs of light:
be still, my heart

raindrops on the bell-rim:
silence sparkles

last light:
lambs cry from hill to hill
the hermit's lamp burns late

rain on a tin roof
but from a deeper sky
the gift of tears

       leafless tree
       in the fold of a hill
       leans into sunrise

someone else's sheep
graze at the hermitage
all one to them

       carcasses in ditches:
       I wintered in the city
       where the rain sounds sweet

lenten vigil
a monk's work-clothes
hang from a nail

       under foot
       generously dunged
       the Pure Land

last minute panic
leaving the hermitage
can't find my watch

[Pure Land: For some Buddhists a heavenly realm, for others, here and now.]

Achill Eagle

(for Grainne)

Floating in a bowl of sky
immensities of sea and mountain
raindrops on a fuchsia's crimson.

Down at Dugort
in ones and twos slow cattle
straggle to the surf-line
bend to the salt
stand doubled in sand-pools

Poised by her easel
she looks and looks again
through the colour
through the form:
swoops when she has seen

In from the rain
a couple of crane-flies
marry their danglings

Larks pipe
over a reedy field
midges are dancing

High up
swifts' hunting-calls
a fly-fisher casts

Still chirping
as a hot day ends
churchyard sparrows

Who's more wide-eyed
        them or us—?
Nest of wild kittens

Purple loosestrife
in the watermeadow
two stray rams

Cows crop short grass
in the chilling air
waft of molasses

First

Darkness felt it.
Up and out. Frost surprises.
The breast of the hill swells with light.
Two red horses blow white breath.
Bowing. Bowing.

Last

A slippered moment out of doors
    finds the strange low light

hears a distant bell-note
    starts to count

but there is nothing beyond one
    opening to gather all

the last
    the lingering

day is night and out
    gives way to in

A Year in South Galway

In the cries of swans
    the winter lake finds voice
        reeds white-feathered

        Behind the north wall
           frost lies undisturbed
               where dogwoods redden

On Brigid's Day
    light through a lattice
        black crosses, blue noughts

        Clouds underwater
           sail through the flooded trees
               their shadows lapping

Exactly this—
    the lustre of a crow
        in April light

        Horizontal sleet
           lights on at noon
               Mayday... Mayday...

The window open
    moonlight fills the room
        with moths' shadows

          Oh quick, the sun
            the fiery sun
               sets beneath the bean-rows

Inhaling meadow-sweet
    a wood-pigeon's two notes
        float upstream

          Wood an-em-on-e!
           offers careful syllables
             as she bends to it

Walking the river-bed
        a long outbreath
its stones
          silent

          Smelling woodsmoke
         in a moment
           summer's autumn

Early days yet:
    along the woodland path
        the crunch of gravel

All day through lovely country
seeing nothing

then a field-gate
held together by rust
the hills through its bars

At the market
voices low and intense
trade gripes

Dare I tell him?
From my neighbour's dungheap
a double rainbow

All night long
my neighbour's dog
guarding the quiet

Smoke-shapes
    brush the stars
the dreaming sow
    groans

At Thoor Ballylee

Swans in winter
float among the trees
heads bowed.

Cold sunlight
casts its shadow-play
upon the walls:

Here the word.
And on his table
Sato's sword

Upstream,
the tumbled mill.
Here bread.

Out back a damson:
fruiting stone.
The sounding water rushes on.

*[Thoor: tower, once the South Galway home of the poet
W.B. Yeats.]*

In the roofless church
the holy-water font
                brimful

                Washing its face
                so very daintily
                a graveyard rat

Hermit's chapel
butterflies are mating
on broken tombstones

                A crow utters
                and the rain replies
                inside a ruin

Beyond the crossroads
the hillroad into autumn
disappears

                Mountain rain
                in this hooded jacket walks
                my ancestor

49

Winter Scroll

Gortnanark—
no-one knows what it means anymore
these empty hills

ask the wind
searching the valley

famine—
pick up any of these rocks
surely it knows

but he is a stranger here
loves the light on red berries

from the woods
the sound of an axe
night falling

The water is pure and cold
murmuring over smooth stones

Such a hush—
are the birds listening?
Pines and their mosses

Dog for company
oil lamp for the long nights

At the Aillwee Caves

Tongue be still
and mind quiet, clear
as a stone pool.

Heart, swell.
Be ample as these caverns,
full of listenings.

Bring here a lifetime's roaring
and say, enough:
here is the living core.

Bow, head and stiff neck,
as a bear, as a deer drinking;

to the kill, and to the gorging;
to the red on snow, to the melting
and to the new green;

the first coming of the upright ones;
and to the last cindered star, bow.

Turning for home
suddenly night
all calls stilled

Almost full moon:
a ladder halfway up the spire
                              paused

On a white road
an old man walks away
into the evening

In a Time of Great Folly

All unknowing
a great work has been in progress.

Opening the door at dawn
there it is, complete.

Sky beyond naming
mired earth made new
the tired track shining.

Of the stillness, and the presence,
who can speak?

The blue rain-barrel
standing slightly askew
its mouth wide open.

ANOTHER COUNTRY

Welsh Rarebit
(for Ken and Noragh)

High seas
in the mirror ceiling
a gull dives

Out-pacing the gulls, the high-speed ferry from Dublin to Holyhead. Fast-food, muzak and slots. Next time I'll walk.

A stowaway
needing no gangplank
to flutter ashore

The country-side around Ty-n-Gors is flat and marshy. St Cybi's Well is nearby. In a reedy field, a cow with long sharp horns licks and licks her calf. Small blue dragonflies dart about the lilypond. A questing red kite glides low.

Effortlessly
into an empty cup
pine-needles fall

We meditate in a farmhouse, bed down in the converted stable. At the evening session, I wonder at some lines from the closing chant: There is nothing to remove and nothing to add. The one who sees the truth of being as it is, seeing this is liberated.

The regime is disciplined but accomodating. Nights after sitting I go to the village pub with Benny. To hear reverence voiced in gravelly Glaswegian is worth the hangover.

Drunk
she dances alone in the bar
nothing to remove

A midge
spirals in sunlight
nothing to add

Travelling on, at Pwllheli station the complexities of the local time-table are more baffling than any sutra, so I phone my host. As it turns out the connections are seamless so I arrive at my destination, where I'm not supposed to be. Two ales and a welsh rarebit later he shows up. Now that's a time-table.

He lives in Cwm Rheidol, a deep glacial valley, thickly wooded. The road into it stops there. The sound of the river fills the coombe. Bedding down in the summerhouse it flows through my dreams.

From the swaying bridge
the weight of a swinging bucket
spilling light

Next morning across the footbridge, up through the woods to the south ridge. The path we follow is an old pilgrim trail to Strata Florida Abbey. Pieties are abruptly dispelled by the piping toot-toot of the narrow-guage train engine swaying by. The windows of its three little carriages bristle with lens.

Snap!
a twig underfoot—
where was I?

There is the hill-fort, commanding Cwm Rheidol and its approaches. What web of farmsteads, currents of hostility and alliance could its ancient builders survey from its heights?

We make for the grove of larches at its foot, a natural grotto in feathery green shade, yin to the fort's yang.

Buzzards wheel above in the late morning blue. Sociable birds, they keep larders in the branches of mountain oak, train their young to drop off into emptiness and soar.

The feel of the place—fort and grove, how they balance and answer each other—soon has us talking of the red thread, raking the embers of loves past. And then fall silent. Our gaze is drawn down into the cwm, to the cauldron where the Rheidol boils.

We are being observed. Through a gap in the slate wall, a young dairy bull the colour of clotted cream regards us with a look of majestic indifference. On his massive forehead the wet hair curls with feminine grace. He radiates primordial force, immovable calm.

> Moonlight Young Prince…
> he stares from a world
> where men are midges.

> In the folds of his muscle
> mountain and meadow, and herd.

Bowing, we move on.

Up and on. My faltering pace quickens with the promise of refreshment. Have I heard right, there's a hotel around the corner?

In the Hafod, cadences of polite English conversation ripple the nineteenth-century atmosphere. There's Coleridge in the corner, reading a borrowed 'Wild Wales'.

> Devil's Bridge—
> a smoking chasm
> cools the air

Rounding the head of the valley to the northern ridge we must detour around the high fences of a hostile settler. Perhaps in time he'll soften, the hard way, when snow and flood teach neighbourliness. Crusties' deserted encampment, wet ash in the fire-pit, pipe-dreams.

Old timers
in the stone circle
    other eyes

Bog cotton—who can come on it fluttering in a lonely place and not feel moved? He tells me of the old custom: impoverished maidens despairing of making a marriage would gather enough to fill a pillow.

We tread warily around the spoil-heaps which disfigure this side of the cwm. Lead mining provided a hazardous means to eke out the meagre earnings of hill farming. But an alchemy of spirit was at work here, I'm told: the silver of theological discussion was their recreation, song their transformative gold.

Rain falls lightly
round a bright orange pool
no birds sing

The light is failing and we're late. At a crossroads, three houses and a public phone-box. He makes the call. As I wait, glancing at the houses, their worn steps and flaking paint, a cat watches from an upstairs window. Two women are talking in a doorway. I can hear every word and, understanding nothing, am absorbed into the sound. A girl comes out and looks shyly across at the stranger. She has a cast in her left eye.

Dripping mist
bog-cotton on barbed wire
maidens' dreams

Something shifts. *The truth of being as it is.* Place and moment gather into completeness. We limp back to Plas Plwca as night falls.

His thin-ness—
two skeletons embrace
departing

One for the Slate
(for Jane and Mickie)

Mountainous slate-heaps tower above the town. Here be giants. From a tangle of mist the old wagon-track, a zigzag of cold lightning, bolts from the summit of Glanypwil and strikes the winding-house below. Wrack and ruin. Here be dwarves.

Early morning: on the main street an aproned woman with a worn kitchen broom unhurriedy sweeps the broad pavement in front of the Queen's Hotel.

> A broken bowl:
> within its jagged rim
> the daily round

In the window of a vacant store the sign Parakeets for Sale/ 2 pair/Good Breeders. The grocer's doorbell tinkles. Newspapers. Bread. Milk.

The bookseller balances an armful of tomes as he struggles with his bunch of keys. Yes he has guidebooks—but could I come back in a while? Make for the heights, find a lake in the clouds.

Blaenau Ffestiniog, boom town once, roofing the world. Nine brothels then, I'm told, a chapel for each, denominations for all, promiscuous proliferation of querulous sects in a landscape of Bethels and Zions, at the bright hem of God. Yet have we sinned: excluded from paradise, the machine in the garden, no place for spoil-heaps in Snowdonia National Park.

Coming down the Inclines, a sheep-farmer berates me in Welsh. I get the message.

> In a maze of back-streets
> follow the sound of running water
> oldest tongue

And stop in at the local. Pint of bitter yer only man. Three men at the bar, one with a West of the Shannon accent. Battler of giants. Disjointed conversation. Industrial accidents. Long pauses.

> In the Manod Arms
> stories of the working dead
> fill an ashtray

Last supper. Pay our respects at the roundstone of Twrog, in a village that feels as though summer lies in its lap, whatever the season. On the menu badger and turnip. The Dwyrdd laps saltily by.

The Dwyryd pool—
a leaping salmon scatters
moonseeds

> Full moon:
> no shadows cast tonight
> the sea-trout play

Chanterelles!
And there two slugs embrace
a stinkhorn

ARAGONESE

Romerías
(for Frank)

night sounds
hearing silence in each creak
and fading footfall

Bedlam at the airport. It seems we all want to leave. Security can't cope. I miss the flight, and ring to say no go. Then I'm on standby. Six hours to explore Departures.

Dispositions of boredom and patience, acceptance and frustration: the stoic reader, the high-pitched cell-phoner, sprawling sleepers, hollow-eyed starers, kids transforming whatever they find, arms outstretched—of course you can fly!

Speechless as a newborn on arrival, wide-eyed, all ears. Over a cerveza, wonder: mother tongue, what is it? All things speak unaided, eloquent in what they are, articulate their being so, sing their story, this, that, thus. Good beer.

The word's gone out. I'm to be met and guided to the train. But how will I know him? Child of the parish, how could I not! Islanders at large, delighting in strangeness. Then gone.

Zaragoza Delicias. Over the Ebro's panflat plain, autumn night air pleasantly warm... now filled with the reek of the paper factory at Mañanas stewing eucalyptus trees from faraway Galicia... *arewethereyet... arewethere yet* ...now Aula Carthuja Dei with its cowled silences and Goya frescos must see them one day. Peña Flor and a barking welcome. We talk into the night.

sunup
the solitary pine
reddens

Consider: enough the yard-brush with its bristles worn on one side; wood-axe leaning on the chopping-block; the water-pump, its handle slick with dew, as if waiting but not so, innocent of name and use, such as they are, radiantly being all their accidental detail, just so.

> rubbing his eyes
> my host in his pyjamas
> needs no telling

Breakfast on local sausage eaten cold, tough-skinned but yielding meaty sweetness, crusty bread dipped in olive oil—and tangy tintos to sharpen our sobriety.

Then to the workshop to see what he's been up to: blocks and columns, lifting-gear, all the tackle of his trade, much of it ingeniously fettled from the scrapheap. On the bench

> armless
> the hero stonily awaits
> *la restoración*

A boy stands in the doorway of a lean-to shed, in a Dublin car dealer's yard piled high with scavenged wrecks. Inside, an old man testing dynamos—much-prized in the trade. He fires-up the starter motor from a battery, sparks fly. The boy marvels and the father smiles, his transmitting-secrets smile. They are one in the mystery of how things work.

But from where the art—the sculptor's eye, the feel for space and volume, the flash of *That?* He has it from his mother's side, they say. Rib of Eve. And there was his Pilar. El Pilar.

Fine white dust. He shows me the fresh-dug grave of his beloved Luna, junkyard dog, her temperament unsafe for all but him. Om mani padma hum. And head north, into the foothills of the Pyrenees. Thought for the road· what man knows his brother? The better part of us is always strange.

2

The way isn't easily found. A bow-legged ancient in the village offers directions. Every year he had climbed to it, but no more. "I'm an atheist myself but these things matter". I ponder his remark as we move on up the mountain. The dog goes nimbly ahead, delightedly nosing.

...arroyo: pleasure of rolling the rrs while I still have mouth-water, picking our way with care along the dry river bed. Unseasonal heat. Begin the ascent. Sierra de Guara, northern Aragon. We are walking on the bottom of the Eocene ocean.

> Simmering in heat-waves
> dream-fish

She stops, bristling. Old fear, a fork in the trail. He calls to her softly: Honey. She comes to heel reassured. A cairn of small rocks sees us right.

Centuries of pilgrimage to a remote cleft in the mountains. *La romeria de la hermita.* Who was he, this hermit? No-one really knows. There is talk of St Martin of Tours whose cult spread south across the Pyrennes but he was no lover of sacred groves. Scourge of druids. No-one knows. And not through piety alone did they come. Legend has it that Aragonese nobles anxious to procure male heirs troubled themselves to climb up here. *La fecundidad.* A rub of the relic.

The zig-zag trail up through pine and prickly holly-oak is gouged in furrows. Wild boar. Rutting, rooting.

Now the rock slope above the tree line: join the dog in scrambling on all fours.

Rosemary and sage, pine nuts in abundance, bilberries in profusion—good hermit fare—honey when he charms the bees with smoky juniper. Good that no-one knows his name, and no church built.

The cleft is in sight. No sound of the fabled cascade, but a haze of water vapour rises, turning rock to cloud.

> eye-level eagle
> playing in the tips of its wings
>   mountain airs

The way's too steep. Honey whimpers. He will stay with her. I should go on alone. *Mi hermano.* He minds me too, his fool elder. We remain together gazing down. It's enough.

Twice, thrice, a bell rings deep in the gorge. Out of the echoes a company of pilgrims appears. Sharing walnuts and pomegranates, we climb down into night.

Over the carpark, the fire-service helicopter clatters to and fro, fetching and dropping water from its little bucket. Each season drier than the last. The groves are burning.

- 3 -

Monasterio Nuevo: comfortably situated in a broad meadow, amply proportioned, seat of princeling churchmen. We tag along on the heritage tour.

> Nothing
> but the best
> in the elegant café
> our just desserts

Cloisters refurbished in the best corporate taste, maple parquet flooring, soft glow of alabaster curtain walls so no harsh light disturb.

> glass floor—
> beneath each fearful footfall
> waxwork monks

They have found peace, and the worm disturbeth not.

Follow the sound of laughter, tinkling glasses. A wedding party streaming to its celebrations. Bobbing along in their wake, a door opens. We find ourselves outside.

Temenos. An open square, at its centre a well.

>   peering up at us
>   two small faces in a sky
>   deeper than the dark

And San Juan of the Rock—where is he in all this 'restoración?' *Abajo: "...low; ground; small, short; pale; faint, soft, low; deep; base; humble; softly, quietly; below..."*

Down the hillside, through the pine-trees and the autumn crocus, lightfoot lads.

Voto, a young nobleman of Z, is hunting in the hills. A deer breaks cover. In hot pursuit, horse and rider plunge into the precipice. A prayer to the Baptist bursts through his terror. He lands safely, by the mouth of a cave. Within, a grieving hermit kneeling by the body of his master, San Juan de la Pena, incorrupt. Having sold all, Voto returns with his brother and enters the life.

Under the belly of the cliff, the original foundation built around the cave, at once pressed down and yet drawn upwards by the rock that threatens and shelters. Chapels and chambers gaunt and tall bearing inscriptions of the kings and queens of Aragon and Ribagorza and, higher than the high, in the rough brickwork of the vaultings, anonymous palm-print of a maker's hand. Dizzying. Look down.

>   in the dust
>   an orchid petal:
>   lightly tread

Hidden in an overhang, a spring drips crystal. Living water wrung
from stone.

        no chanting echoes
        but from the cliffs above
                bees are humming

A Tear of the Sun

Uvas...a word to savour as I push the shopping trolley around the unfamiliar aisles of a Spanish supermarket, stocking up for a week of mountain solitude, in flight from Christmas jingles. Uvas skinned and tinned, stacked high for the celebrations.

> long red nails:
> the checkout girl's a star
> peel me a grape...

Rake out old ash. The wood-stove crackles, settles to a glow. The iron butterfly flutters in its throat with each down-draught of mountain air. In the tiny bedroom the glassy gaze of a long-lashed doll confronts me, chubby arms out-stretched. *Feliz Navidad.* Unquiet dreams.

What day is it? Lose track. Shake loose. Settle.

> mountains
> carried on snow-clouds
> playing light

Perched somewhere up there among the peaks and crevices is the hermitage of San Martín, one of many such *ermitas* scattered in these parts, in their time little lighthouses beaming out across the plain. And though the keepers have deserted the heights, yearly the ancient images are carried up and back from towns and villages, maintaining the delicate balance of sacred and mundane.

Et in arcadia, ego. Burden of longing, obdurate, intractable. The sweetest meat lies closest the bone. Learn stone. Read wood. Study water. Be.

> A feather floats down
> and the load shifts, settles.
> Sometimes that's all it takes.

Last evening. Shower and shave the manimal, walk to the village, see what's cookin' in La Flor. She shrugs. *Sí*. And returns with an armful of firewood. *Jabalí* grilled on the open hearth. To die for.

Perhaps because of the day that's in it—I'd quite forgotten—her man has a treat for me when I go to settle the bill. A glass of his *vino de paga*, on the house. Holds it up, a cloudy rosé, tilted to the light. There—do I see, glistening on the rim? *Lagrima del sol.*

> No grapes at midnight
> but full moon over Moncayo
> is a mouthful

[The story goes that a farmer who had a bumper grape harvest brought his surplus into the town square on New Year's Eve and distributed them free to the revellers, with the suggestion that they eat one for every stroke of the bell at midnight to share in his good fortune.]

Ruta Orwell

Foxy stink
in the ruined fortress
harried even here

In 'Homage to Catalonia' George Orwell writes of the time he spent in these parts with the POUM militia during the Spanish Civil War.

Admiring the pockets of wheat assiduously planted between rocky outcrops, I'm reminded of his observation that in the land which centuries before had perfected the manufacture of steel, the farm implements he saw in use were wooden.

A man of Lacort
harrows his red field
as snow falls

Alcubierre—
spears of winter wheat
break stony ground:

a stand of bearded thistles
guards the pass.

The trenches and sandbagged redoubts are reconstructions but the scouring wind and the sense of melancholy in these hills is real.

Monegros
the heroic struggle against
boredom and lice

Lost kingdoms—
in the dust of Ribagorza
a child's blue glove

Bending to it
the dropped knife
a slice of blue sky

Dinner *alfresco*
serenaded from the rooftop
by a cricket

Too hot to sleep
my companion tonight
a moth in white fur

Cool breeze
fanning the nape of my neck
a wasp's wings

WARRIOR CRIES

Leaf-bursts

Gadom? Can't find it on the map, it doesn't appear on the road-signs, and our taciturn driver is giving nothing away. Yet here we are, gathered in a soft dusk, exchanging welcomes exuberant and shy, familiar faces, forgotten names, fellow retreatants, a babble of tongues.

> frantic guard dog
> life at the end of his chain
> very inviting

> blue cedar
> deepening to black
> full moon

It finds us singly and in animated groups, pensive, lost in argument, tangled in discussion, gathering hurriedly or with mindful tread. In or out it finds us, threatening, inviting. It is time.

> the mis-struck gong
> faithfully strikes
> the striker

Enter.

Can a week have passed - where did it go? Down to the village, perhaps it's there. Spring a little later here, on the level fields a haze of green, daffodils have not yet flowered.

Apartments from the soviet era squat beside crumbling brick barns, greying timber houses. Implements in yards, each eloquent in its own, the broken and the useful, in rain and sunlight, idleness and labour, just as they are. Black soil of vegetable plots, turned and ready.

> the sick cat
> now into ginger fur
> licks warm sun

One shop. The till-keeper's minder enunciates on our behalf. Marl-bo-ro. A few villagers pass, skilled in the art of ignoring. One grizzled brave stops and would speak. Our *dzien dobray* doesn't get us far, and he has less of ours. Yet across the gap of language something arcs. Well met, strangers. Port traffic roars unstoppably past.

> the old road
> cobbles under tarmac
> it too goes nowhere

Between sittings, hens. Every breed and seed of them, picking and pecking, clucking, erupting in clacking consternation, settling again. The crook-backed minder, he too clucks as he moves among them, scattering feed, giving and taking comfort. Keeper of secrets, he has outlived all. Amassed in the barn, artlessly heaped, back-lit by a high window, golden wonders.

Where are we? High ground to the north, rolling woodland and rough pasture, sandy swell of an ancient sea, curious horses. Reed-fringed ponds, cry of duck, deer and fox in the shadows, rumours of wild boar.

And who? *Polens*: people of the fields. Poland, a country that ceased to exist, yet here it is. 'Call me by my real name'. Szcechin/Stettin. Contested identities, occupation, dispossession, disappearance, turn and turn about.

Stumble on the railway line, its dead-straightness cutting a swathe of silence through birch and birdsong. Iron road of hope and fear. What dark-age traffic did it carry to camp or front, escape and exile? In every field a watch-tower.

> peace-time
> shell-casings fall
> from leaf-bursts

Pristine dawn. The guard-dog off his chain ambles in eden, nose wet with dew. Gallus in his apothecary's hat gathers simples—can I say it like that?—for his morning brew: stinging nettle and the bitter herb that heals.

> kind cook
> bent over a whet-stone
> treats his knives

After the feast, famine. Upwelling of wretchedness this morning. Will it ever? Ghosts in sunlight, shadows crystal cut. Look, when looking away brings greater pain. Breathe out. Dissolve.

> the leaning candle
> lends an air of wistfulness
> to the stark shrine

Parting is in the air. And a story told.

> her grief
> in the telling
> we all

Fish break the surface of the muddy willow pond. Dragonflies have hatched. A heron stands unmoved amid reflections.

> the old jetty
> its buckled planks invite
> light feet

That

"...means that might indicate their own invisible and
inexpressible origin..."

Out of nowhere let's say, something:
the arrow of *that* strikes home.

From the hunter's heart
the ruby drop flies.

The world springs up
where it falls.

Ki

Oh fly, little fly
in the crystal of pure appearance
cleaning your legs back and front
your gossamer wings top and bottom
your delicate nose—
how immaculate you are
wherever you land
you take such good care of everything!
Zing—Gone.

So

Bowing
the ground opens up
into the space of a pigeon's call

uhh...huhu...kukuku...
heart syllables
bursting as soft explosions

questing, wide-eyed
utterance of delight, innocence.
Ah! Rise.

LABORARE EST

Yeh Go I

> The slow boy
> gazing skyward
> hears it first

I put down the map and listen with him, hear nothing but trucks and cars roaring past. He stands quite still, looking at me. "You're sure?" "Yeh go I." Ok. A mile or so off the motorway, sure enough we find it, hidden in the hills.

Now the noise is deafening. Boy racers screech around the big circuit in souped-up roadsters. We watch for a while. Cows graze the hillsides undisturbed. Clouds in a blue sky sail out to sea.

Then to the figure-8 go-kart track. Around and around he goes at a sedate pace while I watch. Tiring of it, I go back to the van for a snooze, leaving the attendant to keep watch.

"Good?" He nods, and we're several miles away when I notice he's holding his hand awkwardly. A nasty burn, blistering. He gazes stoically out the window. I can get no explanation out of him. Afraid I won't take him again.

The village pharmacist. Cool-gel and a dressing, painkillers. No, he won't take any payment.

> Healing hands
> where the name itself is balm
> Watergrasshill

Drive on to the seaside. He loves the merries. Yeh go we.

October rain:
the dried-up sapling
puts out spring green

The little larch
still wearing its name-tag
it too turns brown

The old nun
rambling in her mind
must weed the roses

Lengthening
a snail's shadow
draws out the sun

In a biting wind
after the ivy's been stripped
a huddle of snails

Rain at last:
the pebble-dashing snail
goes awol

Seedling

Inch, his few intimates call him when they're feeling fond, and he'll grin wolfishly, and they'll insult each other with warmth and wit, a rueful alliance of the oppressed with the taunted, bolstered by withering contempt for the mongos, pigs and suits they define themselves against.

See him raking leaves on a winter's day, bent to his task, hoodie shadowing his face, he's a diminutive serf locked in the margins of a Book of Hours. See his absorbed expression listening to vintage reggae—he's burnin' babylon.

We sit on the kerb in the nuns' garden. Brief heat draws earthy odours from the leaf-mulch we spread in the rain last week.

There is little can be said. For that reason every word seems weighted. Between them he picks pebbles from the path and flicks randomly. I notice weeds, catch my mind flickering away to plans for spraying, bring it back again. He's talking about drawing, that he'd like to draw. I know this. Does he draw? Nah, can't find the right paper. Rough paper. I suggest a certain shop. Maybe.

> Seedling in gravel:
> plucking it without thinking
> sadness pours out

At dusk
my back stiff from weeding
a marigold's glow

April hail—
two robins at a pear-bud
freeze in mid-fight

This butterfly
has choosen a thistle
to fall asleep on

Something in the Air

> Where does he fly to
> stretched out on the grass
> cloud-rapt ?

"Hey, spacer!" The rude call startles him to his feet, blue eyes wide, sheepish grin his only come-back. And it's on with the work.

We're the boys from the green stuff. With blade and cord and chemical we keep the Great Unruly One in check. Gizza job.

He's on the back-pack blower. A mid-summer storm has torn through Maple Close. Place is a mess. He drives all before him, good leaf-shepherd, master of winds.

Job done, he pauses in the roadway, looks about expressionless. The blower's nozzle swinging idly across the detritus of chippings randomly patterns the underlying surface. He squeezes the throttle gently. Shapes appear and dissolve. Smiles.

> just a few raindrops
> enough to release it
> the fragrance of dust

IN AN ACORN CUP

To a Fallen Swallow

Sweeping round the office park
I find the little *clochán*
fallen from the eaves, its nest
dissolved to mud and straw by winter rain.

The yard-brush stirs the feathered bones and halts:
a light handful you make, slight your remains.
Alive, you'd never let me hold you;
half-ashamed I gaze.

Your red throat—sun-swallower—
amazes, and your bands of blue;
but it's your pert beak—sky-dart—
pierces me.

No cage ever closed around you, pilgrim,
on my open palm your inch-width
stretches without end, your ounce
out-weighs the world.

*[Clochán: a small round hut associated with early
monastic settlement[*

88

Yet another pee
and again the blackbird's watchful
golden eye

Leaves and feathers
patterning the marble tiles
the bare tree silent

Another year ends
and the chirping of small birds
is sweeter than forever

Leaf-drip—
an invisible roofer tap-taps
nails into fog

Twigs aloft—
and him busy at the beam
mouth full of nails

Starlings—
the last one lands
and the whole roof
lifts off

On the Death of an Irish Mountaineer
(for RJN)

The gathering, the scattering...

I should be up there with them
on Maeve's Mountain
but here I am, laid low.

Boot

                hand

                              stick

All day seeing no-one

rock   sky   tree

Then a figure focussing the distance
drawing closer. Stranger; friend.

Up there with them
on Maeve's Mountain:
here I am, laid low.

The crooked mat—
straightening it
a twisted sock

The long evenings—
shouting as they play
tomorrow's ghosts

Planning my moves
to cross the living room
it comes to this

Travelling clock
ticking very discreetly
in the stillness

So fragile, and yet
sheltering an acorn—
parasol mushroom

Wind-lashed bamboo
furiously scribbling
nothings

Garden buddha:
hail rain or shine
same smile

Basho's smile
(for GR)

Years pass, we meet again
between the toilet-paper and the wine;
talk of it—the half-said thing—
as though time were seamless, always now;
then a handshake and we're gone
wheeling down our separate aisles.
Cabbages! Chrysanthemums!
Basho smiles.

Under a cherry tree
the vacant market stall
offers petals

Baristo café:
latest to you live
Iraq with latté

The busker's dirge—
even for his soulful dog
not a cent

Tramlines:
there—where they meet—
that must be It—

Abandoned outside
on a night like this—
an old stove

Evening chill—
what a welcome surprise!
fridge-warmth

Kitchen radio—
voices saying
no-one home

A visitor!
Unfold the cobwebbed chair
it's Hallowe'en

What The Shed-Boy Said

Poor folk about me
'prisoned by their bricks, glazed
and mortar'd-in—what's rain to them,
its music playing leaf & stone—
do they hear the gardens sing?
But worry what the house is worth—
whether to buy, or let, or sell.
Carpet-muffled comes the storm.
The oak above me shakes its crown;
never so many acorns fell.
Last night I heard the vixen scream;
the dogs went wild and bayed a while.
And so I thought—yeh,
blest that in a cabin dwell.

A pink sock
caught up in my greying sheets
the plump laundress

In the curio shop
the lure of old jewellery
for my budding niece

Shyly my nephew
introduces his love:
scented geranium

Ah me!
beauty on a bicycle
her tongue stuck out

Aimless Wandering
[for J&D]

Is that our gong, he wants to know
As Fethard's steeple chimes

And sunlight striking drops of dew
flaming maple, berry-red.

Aimless in the great expanse
at every turn the way appears;

Twisty pine corrects my step
when I fall into straight-line-ness;

The rusty bucket
sets me right, and crow-call says it plain:

The great gong sounds in every sense
wandering the great expanse.

A smile remaining:
the gift came and went
with you

                              Christmas Night:
                              in the Chinese girl's window
                              a longing-lamp

Walking from shadow
his face for a moment sunlit
this stranger

                              Sea fog:
                              a boxful of fisheyes
                              staring at nothing

Sweating as he sweeps
the fish-monger's yellowed ice
into the river

                              Rare fish-flake
                              all the way from Japan
                              for a stray cat

Foghorns

The foghorns are to be silenced.
Who will miss them, mourn their moaning,

care if seacow calls no more to stray calf?
Oh, it'll be a great saving!

Seamen can cope, sailors will steer
by wind-creak, bow-groan.

It's the landsman now who is adrift
and all our lights play false.

Better than bells
they were a proper angelus,

giving pause when lost in busyness,
    drowning in the shallows, pettifogged.

No more now, reminding.

White Eclipse

On solstice day no sun shines in.
The chamber keeps its ancient dark
And the moon is swallowed whole.

And then at noon it snows.
Gravity comes floating down
And everything is white,

Such lightness as lies heavily.

So while it seems I shovel air
From path and drive
I sweat the burden of its levity.

Lit Interior

An angled shaft illuminates
The messy kitchen, and it gleams
As though an excavated shrine;
Enamelled, studded, beaten gold.

Nothing sacred found inside—
Stove and pan, chipped bowl, a spoon—
Nothing holy, yet they glow
Being simply what they are

Lit from surface to interior.

Hiding out
in a snowsuit
mister scarecrow

White silence
at a red traffic light
an empty hearse

A carrot
some pebbles—
he's gone

In a blue china bowl
two boiled eggs
quite naked

Dinner over
in the bowl
one grain

Sound of the spoon
striking the empty bowl:
that's it!